# BASIC ENAMELING

BY Lili Taubes

PITMAN PUBLISHING CORPORATION
New York · Toronto · London · Tel Aviv

# Contents




*Manufactured in the United States of America*

*Library of Congress Catalog Card Number: 74-95903*

*Designed by Anita Karl*

*1.987654321*

# INTRODUCTION

Of all the branches of applied art enameling is surely one of the most rewarding, and this ancient craft is now experiencing a remarkable revival. Working with enamel is exciting and immensely gratifying. There is no finer moment than the experience of seeing a perfectly finished piece emerge from the kiln, and, as the luminous colors slowly cool and solidify, to see the different hues reveal their true beauty. With this in mind, the author here offers the beginner a comprehensive step-by-step method of achieving beautiful results.

## Work Space and the Kiln

For the novice eager to begin, a small space and a very simple outfit will be satisfactory. Kits with all the necessary implements, including a small kiln, can be purchased in most shops that carry artists' supplies. The kiln is an electric furnace used for firing the enamels. Firing is the process of inserting the work into the heated kiln until the enamel is melted. When buying a kiln make sure that it can be plugged into a regular 110 volt electrical outlet. A pyrometer or a thermostat attached to the kiln for automatically retaining a de-

Fig. 1. *Kiln.*

sired temperature is a help but not absolutely necessary—experience and a watchful eye soon teach the enameler when the firing has to be terminated.

As far as working space is concerned, a table covered with a clean sheet of paper that can comfortably hold the basic materials is quite satisfactory. The kiln should stand separately nearby, close to an electrical outlet. Ideally the kiln should be placed on a steel cabinet that contains several shelves where jars of enamel and tools used for firing are kept. If the top of the cabinet is not made of heat-proof material it should be covered with an asbestos plate.

Absolute cleanliness is a must. Metal filings and tiny particles of foreign matter will damage your enamel work.

# Metals Used for Enameling

Enamel work is done on metals exclusively. A variety of these can be used for this purpose—copper, silver, gold, and others. Copper is the most practical; it is easy to work on, economical, and can be bought either in sheets or in ready-made shapes such as trays, plaques, pins, and pendants. It is advisable to choose 18 gauge copper. Gauge is the term used to define the thickness of metal; the higher the number of the gauge, the thinner the metal. Silver also provides a fine metal base for enamels, especially as background for the brilliance of such transparent colors as green, blue, and purple. But it is much more expensive and not quite as easy to handle as copper. Enameling on other metals requires a great deal of experience and should not be attempted by the beginner.

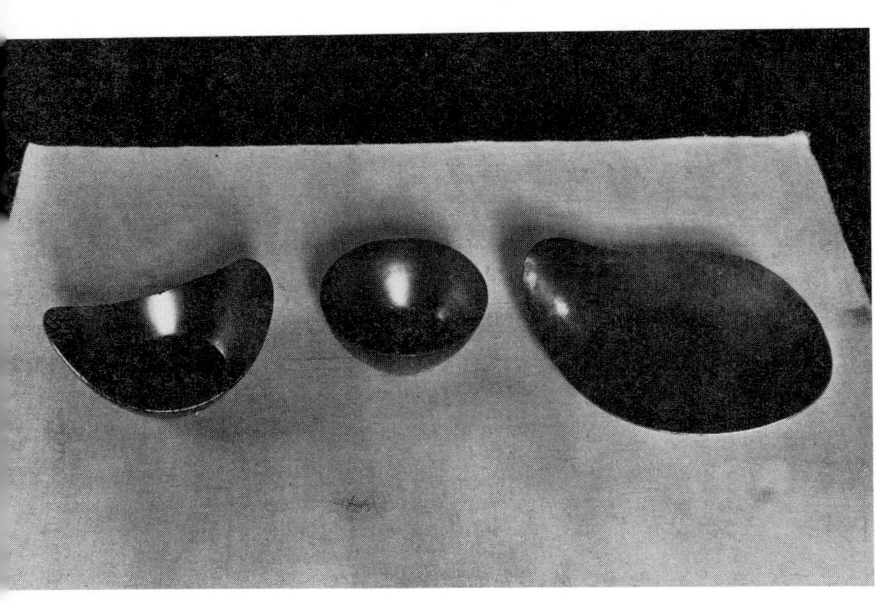

Fig. 2. *Copper trays for enameling.*

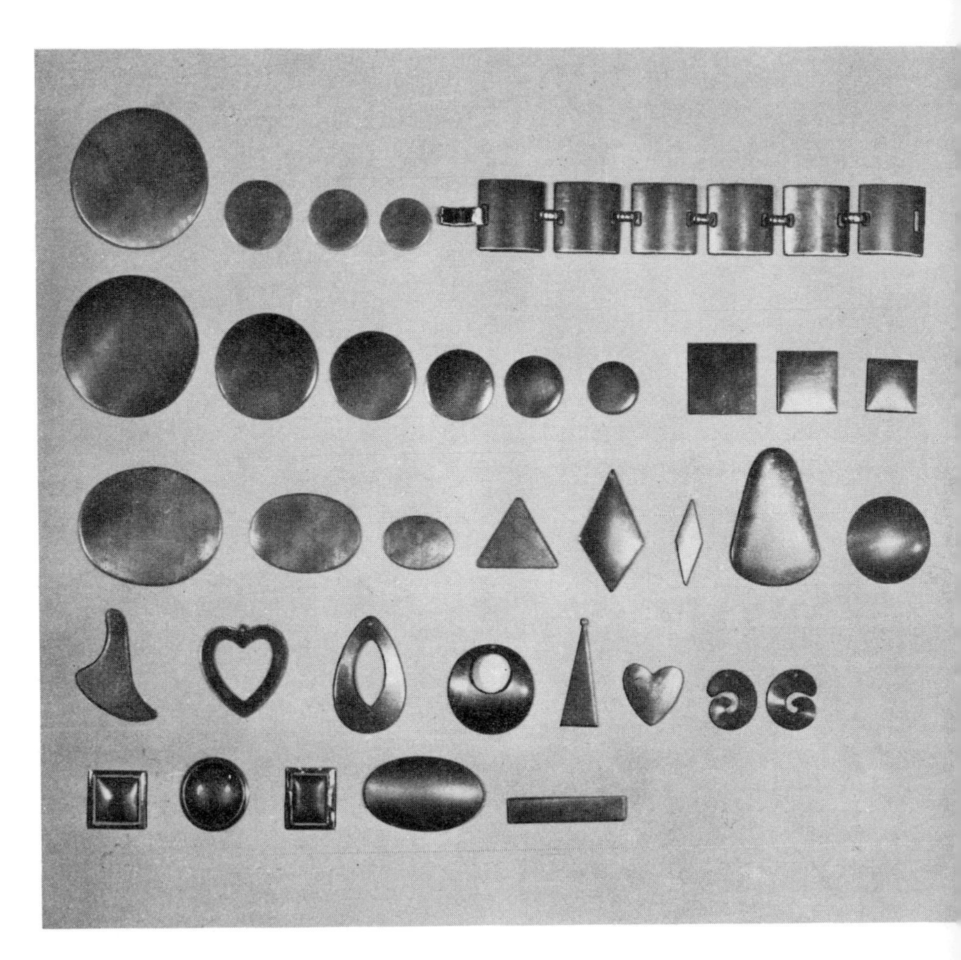

Fig. 3. *Ready-made copper and silver shapes for enameling.*

# Enamels

ENAMEL IS MADE by compounding various minerals like feldspar and silica. It is a vitreous material which can be fused onto a metal foundation in a kiln. Enamels are produced in different grades of hardness—the harder the enamel the higher the melting point needed to result in a glasslike surface. Enamels can be bought in powder form, ready for firing, in a countless variety of shades, and in three types: opaque—the undercoat or metal does not show through, translucid or semitransparent, and transparent—the undercoat or metal shows through. In the last category belongs *flux*, a waterclear colorless enamel which is available in three grades—soft, medium soft, and hard.

The enamel colors should be kept in glass jars with mesh screens and tight fitting tops. Glass jars with 80 mesh screen tops are recommended for regular use. (Mesh means the number of openings on a square inch of the metal sifter through which the enamel is dusted onto the object.) 250 mesh sifts the enamel almost as fine as face powder. This is best suited for delicate work, like the Limoges technique. Glass jars already provided with a mesh screen allow the colors to be sifted directly from the jar, thus protecting the enamel from impurities.

# Color Charts

TO BECOME ACQUAINTED with the characteristics of individual colors you may want to produce your own charts. The charts are a great help because many powdered enamels look quite different in the "raw" state than they do when baked. Prepare the charts as follows: take three oblong copper strips; leave one bare but polished, cover one with clear flux, and cover the third with pure white enamel. The two strips covered with enamel have to be fired in the kiln. Follow the firing procedure described in the following paragraphs. Then set small patches of the same colors next to each other on every strip. All three strips are then fired. Now you have the same colors on various backgrounds—flux, white, and polished copper. You will see marked differences in the colors that have been fused to different backgrounds. Finally, number the color patches with watercolor and give the charts a quick burning to fasten the numbers.

It is important to know that an object always has to be fused over with a basic layer of enamel first before being decorated. Opaque pure white and flux are very good choices for background, because both show colors used over them to their best advantage.

# THE BASIC ENAMELING PROCESS

THE KILN is plugged in. It will take approximately 45 minutes to heat to about 1200° and up to 1400° Fahrenheit; the inside will be uniformly glowing red. The following materials should be lined up on the working table:

*Two metal objects* to be enameled, preferably small 18 gauge copper plaques, ovals about 1½ inches by 2 inches, slightly domed. Domed means raised in the center, thus not completely flat. It is not only more fun to prepare two pieces at a time, it also is a form of practice, and an opportunity to experiment. Later on you may wish to have a choice of different copper shapes which already have a base coat. A flat transparent box lined with soft blotting paper is excellent for storing such enameled forms ready to be decorated.

*Enamel colors* for foundation layers. Waterclear flux and pure solid white are good choices.

*Sifter.* This can be eliminated if the enamel is sifted directly from the jar through an 80 mesh cover. Although sifting from a jar is practical for enameling small objects, the use of a separate sifter is recommended for covering larger surfaces.

FIG. 4. *Box with enamel plaque on cover.*

*Klyr Fyre* or *Gum Tragacanth.* Both are faintly sticky adhesives that make the enamel adhere to the metal.

*Carborundum stone* for smoothing rough edges of the metal.

*A soft brush* to apply the adhesive.

*Scalex.* A medium to protect the bare, unenameled metal from oxidation.

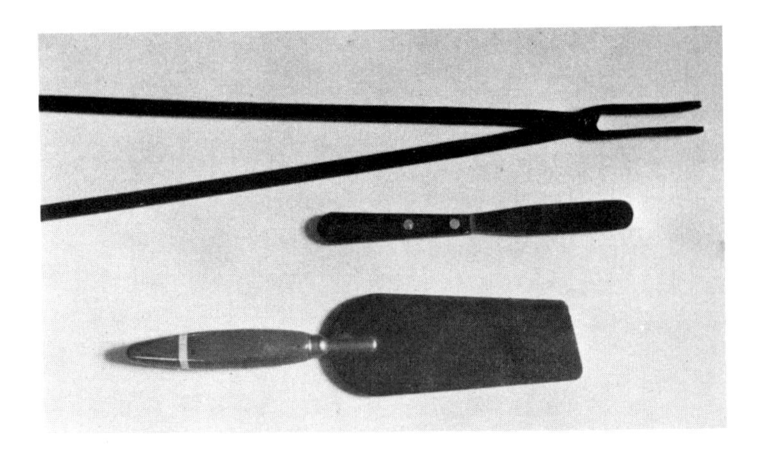

FIG. 5. *Top: Tongs. Bottom: Spatulas.*
*Used for handling hot enamels.*

*Long metal tongs* preferably made of stainless steel. They are used for handling the work before and after firing.

*Asbestos gloves* to protect your hands from the heat. Remember, the kiln and your enameled object get very hot!

*Soft white blotter.*

*Clean sheets of paper.*

*Steel wool.*

*Small round sable brush.*

*Large and small spatula* made of stainless steel for handling and lifting the hot enamel after baking.

*Hard asbestos plate.*

*Findings* like enamel threads, tiny balls, gold and silver foil, for decorating the piece. This is the final phase, after the base coat of clear flux or white opaque has been fused to the object.

# Procedure

STEP 1. The metal has to be scrupulously cleaned before the enamel is applied. Cleaning should be done with steel wool, soap, and scouring powder; this should be sufficient. If there are still impurities noticeable on the surface, the piece should be immersed in pickle, a metal cleaning agent which can be bought in an art supply store. Slight heating hastens the cleaning process. When the metal looks flawlessly clean, hold the metal by the edges only, rinse it thoroughly, shake the water off, and place it on a clean blotter. Never touch the surface that has to be enameled with your fingers. Fingermarks mean grease and dirt, the worst enemies of enamel work. The enamel will not stick to metal with fingerprints.

STEP 2. Spread a clean sheet of paper on the table, large enough to catch surplus enamel—about 15 inches square. A separate sheet must be used for each color.

Fig. 6. *Pouring the enamel powder from the jar into an 80 mesh sieve. The cover is kept underneath to avoid waste.*

Now, lift the cleaned plaque with a spatula and hold it at the edges—don't touch the surface! Brush a coat of Scalex onto the back. Don't get any of this material on the upper surface, because enamel will not cling to these spots. Put the plaque down for the Scalex to dry and repeat the same procedure on the second piece.

Step 3. Now the kiln has been heated to the proper degree and the Scalex has dried. Have the enamel handy, either in a mesh top jar or in a sieve. If you pour the powder into a sieve put the jar cover beneath it to avoid waste. Before the basic layer of enamel is applied to the object, lift it at the edge and paint a thin coat of Klyr Fyre or Gum Tragacanth on the top surface. This substance makes the powdery enamels adhere to the metal surface. Then, from a distance of about 5 inches above, dust this surface with enamel, either by gently moving your wrist or tapping the sieve with a finger. See to it that the powder falls evenly in an easy flow. The plaque should be moved and tilted slowly so that the whole surface is evenly covered.

Fig. 7. *Dusting the metal object with enamel from about 5 inches above.*

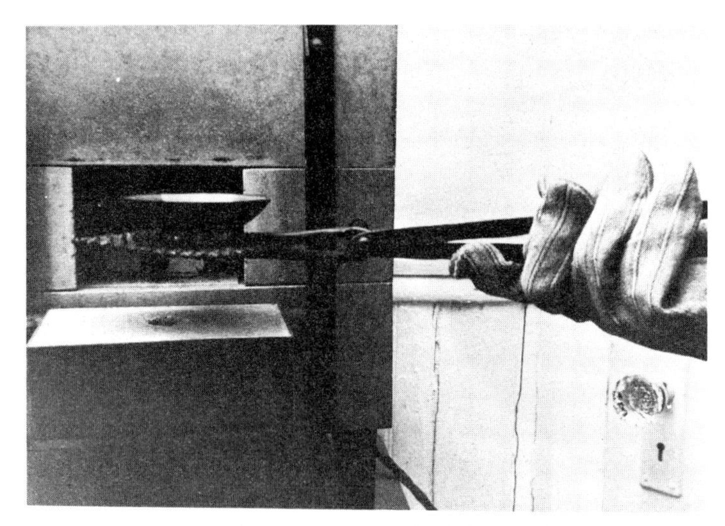

Fig. 8. *Putting the piece into the kiln for firing.*

Step 4. With the help of a spatula, place the plaque on a wire mesh screen and, using the long metal tongs to hold the screen, your hand protected with an asbestos glove, cautiously place the plaque in the kiln. Repeated peeping into the oven gives you the first exciting experience of seeing the enamel change from the raw gritty stage into a glowing, glassy surface. Firing time takes about 1½ to 3 minutes, and sometimes even more, depending on the hardness of the enamel. Enamel goes through several stages very quickly when in the kiln.

Step 5. After the enamel has melted into a glasslike surface, the work is immediately pulled from the kiln, following the same instructions as putting the piece into the kiln, and using caution. Remember, your object and the kiln are red hot! Then, using a spatula, remove the object from the wire mesh and place it face down on a hard asbestos board. With a wide spatula, press down on the object to prevent warping. A spatula is advised for small objects; larger ones should be weighted down with a flatiron.

Step 6. There may be flaws after the first baking. Bare dark spots on the surface of the plaque indicate that the layer of enamel was too thin—the dark spots represent the bare copper oxidized by fire. After your work cools these have to be carefully removed with steel wool. Also, the blackened rim will have to be treated with a fine file. Move the file in one direction only—away from the enameled surface. After all traces of fire scale are removed, rinse the piece thoroughly, and dry it with a clean blotter. Should "bald" spots appear, they have to be covered with enamel again. Before the second firing, make sure that the Scalex on the reverse side is intact. Most enamels will need three or four firings of one to three minutes each before the piece is finished.

If you followed instructions carefully you now have two enameled objects with perfect foundations ready to be decorated.

STEP 7. Let us start with the oval that was fused over with white as the foundation layer. Dust the white plaque with a bright transparent color. Then, using tweezers, choose a number of interesting shapes like dots, enamel strings, and tiny balls from the findings and, using your imagination, arrange them on the plaque in an attractive irregular pattern. Do not disturb the fresh layer of enamel. Then, using tongs and gloves, place the piece in the kiln and watch the melting enamel carefully. When it is smooth and glossy, remove the work from the kiln. Make sure that it cools slowly. Sudden temperature changes can cause the enamel to crack. Then clean the reverse side and polish it, as well as the rim, with steel wool. Your first enamel piece is now finished.

FIG. 9. *Enameled pin decorated with findings.*

After familiarizing yourself with these fundamental processes, you may wish to broaden your experience and your knowledge of the craft. In the following pages you will learn about four specific types of enamel work: Painted enamel, which includes Sgraffito and Limoges, Cloisonné, Repoussé, and Champlevé or Bassetaille.

Fig. 10. *Enameled trays in paint technique.*

# PAINTED ENAMEL

Painted enamel is the term given to the most frequently used technique of enamel work. It refers to painting with the enamel material.

Fig. 11. *Earrings in paint technique (actual size 1¼ inches).*

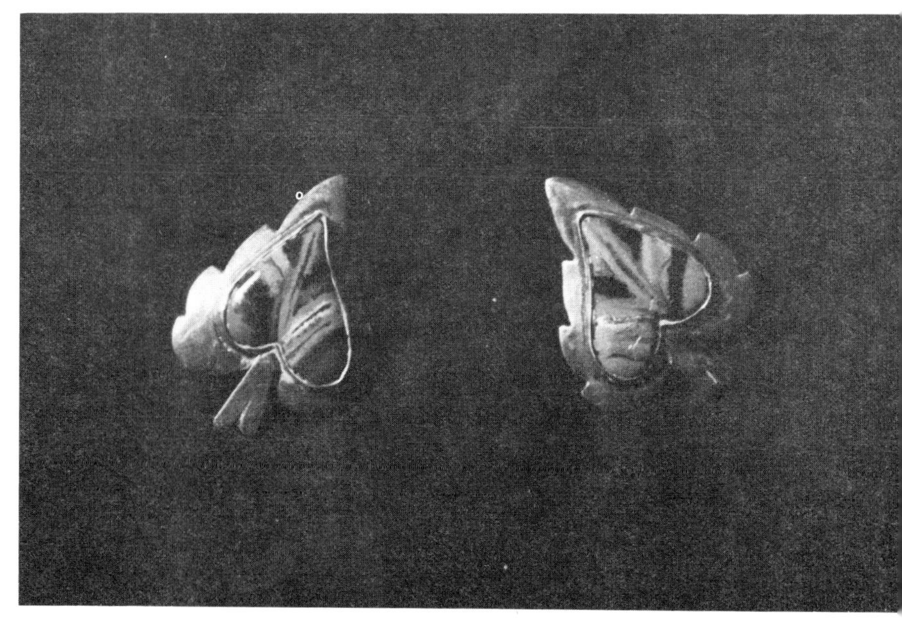

# Preliminary Procedure

THERE IS ONE DIFFERENCE in preparing the objects for this technique. Now both sides of the metal should be coated with enamel, which on the reverse side is called "counter enamel." This is done to reduce tension and possible cracking of the upper surface enamel after repeated firings of the piece, and to avoid annoying fire scale on bare parts of the copper. Counter enamel also gives the work a more finished, substantial appearance, and in addition the reverse side can be decorated.

To prepare objects for the painted enamel technique, hold a very thoroughly cleaned metal object at the edges with your fingers—don't touch the surface! Begin with the reverse side, in order to obtain a flawless upper surface. First, it is brushed with Klyr Fyre or Gum Tragacanth. Immediately after, enamel is sifted over the surface. Then, gently—no jerking—the piece is turned over for the same process. It is then baked in the kiln, following the instructions on page 10.

Bits of surplus enamel should be collected together in a special jar. This mixture results in an agreeable grayish shade well suited for counter enamel. A pure white color is preferable when transparent or translucid colors are being used over the foundation layer because it brings out other shades so well.

The following materials should now be available for the painted enamel technique:

*A copper object,* preferably a small plaque or a tray, which has previously been given a basic coat of enamel and baked as described in the previous paragraphs.

*A set of small flat trays or dishes* of china or plastic. The kind that can be stacked are best.

*One or two small round brushes,* made of sable hair.

*A soft clean blotter.*

*A preliminary watercolor sketch on paper* using the colors you have chosen. This will be helpful in planning the design. The design can be very simple, geometrical or in the shape of a leaf or flower. An outline can be marked with watercolor directly on the enameled surface.

*Two or three colors.* It is advisable to use only a few at first.

FIG. 12. *Mortar and pestle for grinding enamel to a finer grain.*

# Procedure

FIRST, the colors have to be made ready for use. Place small amounts of each shade you plan to use into a separate shallow tray. For this type of work 80 mesh is usually the desired fineness. If a finer powder is desired, it has to be ground down in a mortar with a pestle. After the enamels are ground down (this will take a few minutes), they too are placed in small dishes. Then the enamels have to be washed. Slowly fill each little dish containing enamel with water. Gently tap the dish, and the fine enamel powder will settle to the bottom. The milky slush that stays on top has to be poured off. Repeat this procedure until the water is clear. The trays are then lined up on the working table and work can begin.

The enamel colors, moistened with water, are applied directly onto the enameled surface of the object in small portions with a fine round sable brush. Surplus water is soaked up with a blotter that is held to the edge of the piece. After all the colors have been applied, the moist enamel must be carefully dried. This is best done on top of the kiln. Wet enamel put into the hot kiln will pop off.

The first baking should be short, that is, just long enough to make the enamel paint fuse. The duration of the firing process depends on the hardness of the enamel. A softer enamel may fuse in 1½ to 2 minutes, a harder enamel may take 3 minutes. Watch your piece carefully while it is in the kiln. Repeated firings of the piece will most likely follow to correct flaws and add finishing touches.

FIG. 13.

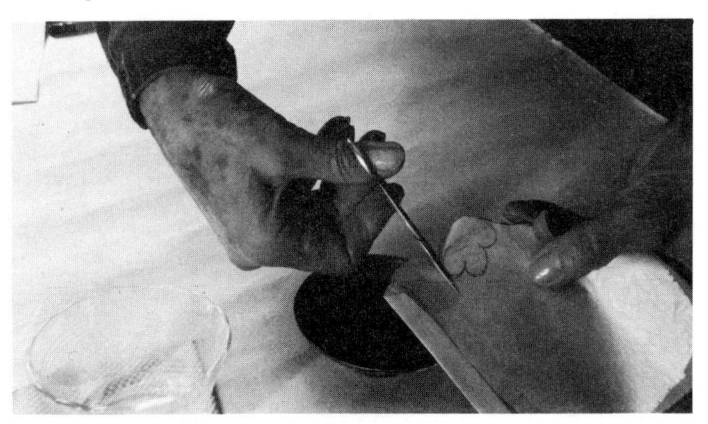

Details like shading and fine outlines can be added by using very finely ground enamel. Lavender oil is used instead of water as the painting medium for these fine enamels. They should be applied before the last firing because the delicate shades can fade when exposed repeatedly to the high heat of the kiln. A detailed description of the treatment of delicate colors can be found in the section on Limoges technique, page 26.

## Foils

GOLD AND SILVER FOILS are often used with painted enamel, and can be bought in sheets especially suited for enameling. They are very effective as underlay for transparent colors. For example, blue, green, and purple are beautiful over silver foil, and gold foil adds brilliance to transparent red. To use foil, place the delicate sheet between two layers of tissue paper on which the outline of your design has been sketched. Carefully cut with small scissors (see fig. 13). Next dampen the area where the foil is going to be placed. Then lift the foil with a

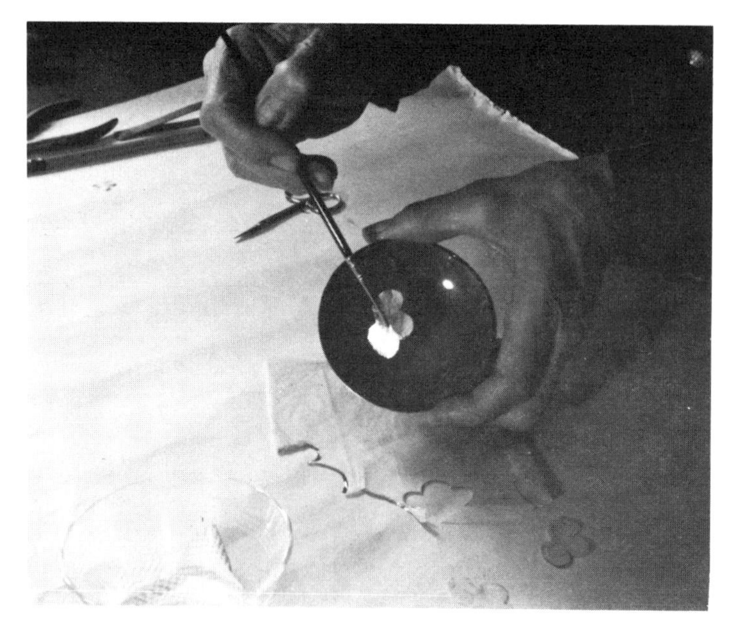

Fig. 14.

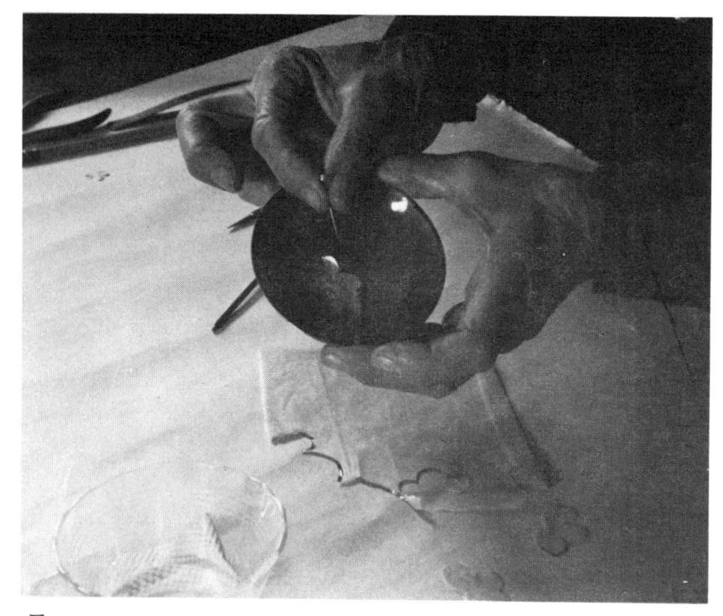

Fig. 15.

slightly moistened sable brush and place it on the object (see fig. 14). Next, prick the foil with a fine needle (see fig. 15). This lets air escape during firing and the foil will bake on flat. After a short firing the foil will fuse to the foundation. It is then covered with a transparent enamel.

There are also so-called *metallic lustres* on the market. They are not made from precious metals, and are reasonably priced. When painted on and lightly fired, they are very effective as finishing touches.

Fig. 16. *Here the foil is seen with the watercolor sketch.*

Fig. 17. *Brooches and pendant using gold and silver foil.*

# SGRAFFITO

Sgraffito is an ancient pottery technique which has been adapted for enameling. It is relatively simple to execute, quite effective, and well suited to adorn trays and covers for decorative boxes.

## Materials Needed

*Slush,* an enamel in liquid form.

*A brush* or *sprayer.*

*A metal object*—copper tray or plaque.

*Enamel* for base layer in powder form.

## Procedure

The object to be decorated is first fused over with enamel of any chosen color. After cooling, a layer of slush, which can be bought ready for use, of any *opaque contrasting* shade is brushed or sprayed over the

Fig. 18. *A line drawing is scratched out of the top layer of enamel. Here it has been done with a "comb" cut from a piece of cardboard.*

basic enamel. Then a line drawing is scratched out of the slush, revealing the color of the underlying surface of enamel. The pointed wooden end of a paint brush is well suited for doing this. A wide pronged fork can also be used to create a rhythm in the design. The object is then fired. Decorative touches such as shading and glazing with finely ground paint enamel can be added, as well as tiny lumps and strings of enamel, or metallic ornaments that can be bought ready-made. Metallic ornaments should be fused over with soft flux for protection.

After having acquired some practice in handling enamel colors, you may wish to explore more complex projects. The next step is to try your skill on Cloisonné.

Fig. 19. *The rim of the finished piece is filed clean from black fire oxidation.*

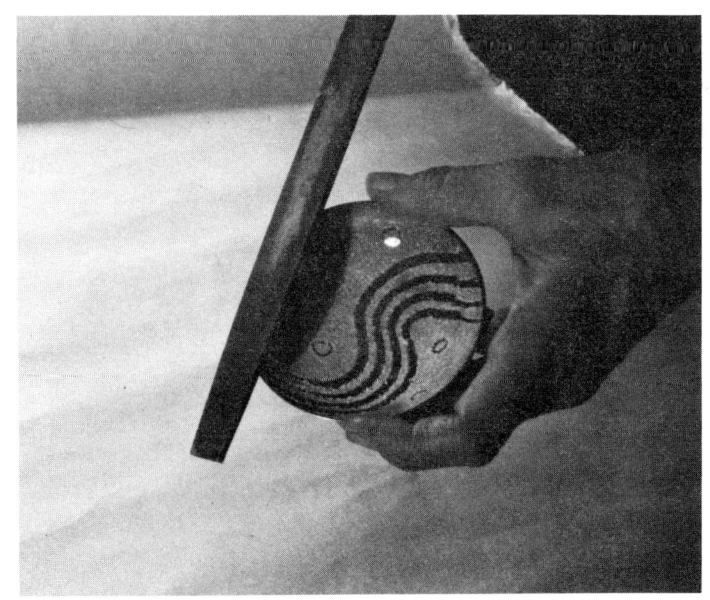

# CLOISONNÉ

CLOISONNÉ is essentially related to painted enamel, with one important difference. The colors are not set directly next to each other. They are separated by a net, or cells of thin wire, called cloisons.

## Materials Needed

*A prepared metal base,* preferably copper, which has been covered with a layer of medium soft flux. A flat plaque is best for the first attempt.

*Silver cloisonné wire.* This is a kind of flat wire, 1/32 inch by .008 inch. It can be purchased at an art supply store especially for this purpose.

*Small tweezers and pliers,* used to bend and shape the wire forms.

*A small snip,* which is a small shears for cutting wire.

*Enamel colors.* Choose colors with the same melting point.

*A fine brush, spatula,* and *spreader* for filling the wire cells with enamel.

*Carborundum stone, steel wool, blotter.*

FIG. 20. *Eleventh century Byzantine plaque in cloisonné technique.*

*A preliminary sketch on paper,* to avoid confusion and technical difficulties during work. The design should also be faintly outlined with watercolor on the plaque.

FIG. 21. *Shaping the wire according to the sketch on paper.*

# Procedure

WHEN PLANNING a design for Cloisonné, long straight lines should be avoided. Small curved or bent shapes are easier to follow and execute with the wire.

Shape the wire with small tweezers or pliers, following the outlines of the design on your preliminary sketch. Use a snip for cutting, and place the pieces onto the paper sketch. When all the pieces are assembled and satisfactorily arranged, pick them up piece by piece with the tweezers and dip each into a watery solution of Gum Tragacanth. It acts as an adhesive and keeps the

FIG. 22. *The wire shape is now ready to be cut off with the snip seen in the foreground.*

Fig. 23. *The wire shape is dipped into a solution of watery Gum Tragacanth and placed onto the prepared plaque which has been fused over with flux.*

Fig. 24. *Wires fused onto an enameled pin.*

wire pieces, which are put upright on the flux ground, in place. A short firing follows, just long enough to fuse the wires to the enamel base. In case a few wires are not quite attached to the flux, gently press them down with a wide spatula.

After the piece has cooled, the cloisons or wire cells are filled with water-moistened enamel. (Hard enamels, the ones with a high melting point, are not suited for this technique.) Use a small brush or spatula to fill the cloisons, and a spreader to push the enamel carefully into all corners of the wire shapes. Blot off surplus water. When all the cloisons are filled, *dry the work very thoroughly on top of the kiln.*

Fig. 25. *Finished cloisonné pin.*

Fig. 26. *Twelfth century Byzantine jewelry in cloisonné technique.*

The firing that follows should be long enough to melt the colors. After this, there may be flaws, hollows, and uneven spots; they have to be recharged with enamel. Sometimes this procedure has to be repeated a few times. Before the last firings, remove all uneven spots by grinding them with carborundum. This is best done under running water to float off all removed matter. After the final firing the work should leave the kiln with a smooth and shiny surface.

# REPOUSSÉ

Repoussé is a technique in which the enamel is fused onto a metal foundation that has been worked into a relief from the reverse side. Examples of this technique are found mostly in museums. They are interesting, not too complicated to produce, and a challenge to the enterprising enameler.

## Materials Needed

*A piece of copper,* the size of the planned design.

*A stylus,* a penlike metal instrument with a blunt, pointed end. Also, one with a rounded end.

*Layers of stacked paper,* to rest the metal on while working on it.

*Transparent enamel.*

## Procedure

Choose a piece of copper thin enough to yield to the pressure of the stylus, about gauge 22. Place the metal on the layers of paper or another foundation soft enough to "give" when the tool presses on it. First, outline the design lightly with a needle on the back of the metal surface, then emboss it with the stylus. Embossing means to raise the surface of a design into a relief. Remember, this is achieved by working on the reverse side. A stylus with a rounded end can be used in addition to produce a greater variety of texture and pattern. More or less pressure is used according to the desired depth of the relief. (The more pressure you put on the stylus, the greater the height of the relief on the right side.) Since all the work is done on the back of the piece, check the front frequently to see whether the result is satisfactory. The pressure of the tool should be gradual and light enough to allow for corrections.

Fig. 27. *Finished plaque. The relief has been covered with a transparent enamel.*

After the relief is finished, it is thoroughly cleaned and carefully polished with fine steel wool to a high sheen. Then it is sifted over with a layer of soft transparent enamel of light color, and a short firing follows. A variety of shades, all light and transparent, can also be applied. Light blues and greens are fine covers if a silver plaque has been chosen for the background. The pattern of the relief shimmering through the enamel is very effective.

It is not necessary to apply counter enamel to a Repoussé relief, although a layer of enamel—preferably the same color as on the right side, gives added support to the thin metal. If copper (not silver) is used for the relief, and no enamel is put on the reverse side, the bare copper has to be brushed with Scalex to prevent fire scale from forming.

# LIMOGES

Limoges is a technique in which the design is gradually built up with very finely ground enamels between successive firings. It gives the impression of a dainty relief. This interesting technique is closely related to the category we called painted enamel, but it demands more experience and skill in handling the enameling material. It is very well suited for small pieces like jewelry.

FIG. 28. *Limoges.*

## Materials Needed

*White enamel,* very finely ground, about 250 mesh.

*Oil of lavender.*

*Frosted glass plate* about 8 inches square.

*A muller.*

*A small spatula* with a straight end.

*Fine small round brushes.* Sable is best.

*An object to be decorated.* It is advisable to begin with a small plaque, about 2 inches by 2 inches, slightly raised, previously fused over with a dark transparent layer of enamel. The white limoges decor looks best on a dark transparent color.

# Procedure

SOME ENAMELERS begin with a preliminary sketch done on the prepared plaque, as follows: A minute portion of the very finely ground enamel powder is moistened with water, like a watercolor, and with this the planned design is thinly and evenly sketched onto the background. After it has dried, a short firing follows, just long enough to fasten the design to the background. It will be faint but clear enough to follow.

Now the enamel has to be prepared for the actual build-up. A small portion, about a scant teaspoon, of the fine white enamel powder is put onto the frosted glass plate and moistend with lavender oil. It is then ground with a muller to a soft paste and, when it attains a soft consistency, pushed into a small heap with a spatula. It has to be kept immaculately clean, free from lint and dust, tightly covered when not in use. Depending on the consistency of the white enamel paste, that is, used thickly or thinned with added oil, you can achieve shades from grayish transparency to pure white opaque impasto.

The design is then painted on with very fine round sable brushes between *successive* firings so that it gives the impression of a distinct relief. It is important to know that any object painted with this type of enamel has to be "smoked off" before every firing, which means it has to be held in the warmth of the open kiln door until the volatile oil has completely evaporated. During the smoking off process, the white shiny limoges color becomes dull and yellowish. It can then be put into the kiln. It becomes white and glossy again during the firing. The firing period has to be carefully checked to prevent overburning—remove the work from the kiln the moment the design appears glossy.

Very finely ground enamels are also available in a variety of shades. They can be used for tinting the white limoges relief design before the last firing. The paint medium for these colors is also oil of lavender.

# CHAMPLEVÉ

Champlevé is a technique in which enamel is filled into recesses on the surface of the object. These recesses are made either by etching or engraving. Splendid examples of this type of enamel work can be seen in museums, and the technique can be effectively adapted for modern design.

## Materials Needed

*Flat metal plate,* preferably copper, about gauge 16, in the size fitting the planned design.

*Etching ground,* which can be purchased ready for use at an art supply store.

*Nitric acid* for etching, diluted in water. The ratio is one part acid to two parts water. Always pour the acid into the water, never the other way around! Nitric acid is highly corrosive. Hands and garments should be protected when using it and you should avoid inhaling its fume. *Iron chloride,* a non-corrosive etching medium, can be used instead of nitric acid. No special care is necessary in handling it, but the etching process is much slower with iron chloride. Nitric acid will take approximately one to two hours, whereas iron chloride may take four hours or more.

*Scraper, steel wool, carborundum, turpentine, flat pan.*

*Enamels, brush.*

*Wooden tongs,* used when handling objects submerged in acid.

## Procedure

*Etching* is the preferred method for making recesses in the metal surface. Before etching, brush the metal plate evenly with the etching ground. The etching ground will preserve the parts of the surface that you want to protect from the acid. When dry, scratch an outline of the design lightly onto the the surface of the etching ground with a needle. Then scrape the etching ground off the areas to be etched, that is, the areas you want exposed to the acid. After this is done, the plate is submerged in a shallow glass or plastic pan containing the acid, and left there until all the exposed parts are eaten away to the desired depth, that is, deep enough to be charged with enamel. Check the progress of the etching frequently. This is done by attaching a piece of cotton to the wooden end of a brush and moving it gently over the surface of the object sub-

Fig. 29. *Etched metal shapes, ready to be filled with enamel.*

merged in the acid to remove residue of metal exposed to the acid.

When the etching is finished, remove your work using the tongs and rinse the piece thoroughly.

Now the remaining etching ground is removed with turpentine, and every trace of it thoroughly scrubbed off. Next, the recessed parts are covered with enamel, carefully dried, and fired. After the first baking, the enamel surface may not be flush with the elevated level of the metal. If it has high spots or hollows, it has to be ground to an even surface. This is done, after the piece cools, with carborundum stone under running water to float off all loose particles. Also, remove traces of enamel from the bare copper parts. Then the uneven spots are recharged, the piece dried and put into the kiln again. If there are still flaws, the grinding, recharging, and firing has to be repeated until the work leaves the furnace with an even and glossy surface. Then the metal part is polished with fine steel wool to a high sheen.

Plique-a-jour is a technique in which the enamel sometimes appears without a metal background, thus giving the impression of stained glass. We will not be discussing it in this book because the whole procedure requires knowledge of metal work. Ready-made cast silver shapes for small pieces can be obtained for this type of work.

# HELPFUL HINTS

1. Patience and neatness are important. Hasty, untidy work often causes failure and disappointment.

2. Colors should always be tightly covered when not in use.

3. Have a notebook handy to jot down appealing effects and compatible color combinations.

4. Fuse small individual samples of colors onto tiny patches of metal. Fasten them to the jars with tape and keep a record of their precise number and hardness.

5. Label jars clearly with name and number, and state whether the color is opaque or transparent. This will prevent errors and waste; it is also useful in case of repeat orders.

6. Leftover bits of enamel should be collected together in a special container. The mixture results in a neutral shade and can be used as counter enamel on the reverse side of objects.

7. In planning a design, make a preliminary watercolor sketch to assure a well-balanced design.

8. Try different textural effects using beads, tiny balls, gold and silver stars, dots, and other ornaments. These, as well as liquid metals which can be painted on as finishing touches, can be bought ready-made.

9. Opaque pure white and waterclear flux are good choices for background as most colors painted on them appear to their best advantage.

10. Color charts are very helpful to distinguish the appearance of an enamel in the "raw" state from its appearance when fired.

11. A piece of mica, easily removable, put inside on the bottom of the kiln, prevents bits of enamel which may drop from your work from fusing to the kiln.

12. Enamel work has to be warmed up before each repeated firing. The enamel will crack if exposed to sudden high temperature.

# GLOSSARY

*Asbestos*—A mineral used for making heatproof and fireproof articles.

*Carborundum*—A synthetic abrasive stone used for grinding and smoothing metal and enamel.

*Champlevé*—A process in which the enamel is fused into recessed parts of a metal foundation.

*Cloisonné*—A process in which enamel fills wire cells or mesh.

*Counter Enamel*—Enamel covering for the back of an object.

*Emboss*—To raise the metal surface of a design into a relief, working from the back.

*Emery Cloth*—A cloth prepared with an abrasive.

*Enamel*—A glasslike material that can be fused to a metal foundation using heat.

*Etching Ground*—A dark brown bituminous substance applied to metal to protect parts from the effect of acid in the etching process.

*Flux*—A waterclear transparent enamel.

*Foil*—Very thin sheets of metal in gold or silver especially prepared for enamel work, used for decorative purposes.

*Gauge*—A standard measuring instrument, used to determine the thickness of metal.

*Gum Tragacanth*—A flaky substance that, when soaked in water, yields a slightly sticky liquid.

*Impasto*—Paint laid on thickly.

*Iron Chloride*—A noncorrosive etching medium.

*Kiln*—A furnace or oven used for enamel work.

*Lavender Oil*—A fragrant oil, used as a paint medium for very finely ground enamels.

*Limoges*—A technique in which the design is gradually built up with very finely ground enamels between successive firings to give the impression of a relief.

*Mesh*—The number of openings to a square inch of the sieve used to shake enamel on the object, thus determining the fineness of the powder.

*Mica*—A mineral used in thin heat resistant sheets, to prevent enamel from fusing onto a support.

*Mortar*—A bowllike vessel in which enamel can be reduced to a finer grain with a pestle.

*Muffle*—The inner part of the kiln, where the work is placed for firing.

*Muller*—A glass implement with a flat base for grinding enamels to extreme fineness on a frosted glass plate, that is, glass with a roughened surface.

*Nitric Acid*—A corrosive acid with powerful etching action. Always pour the acid into water in the proportion of 1:2.

*Opaque*—Not transparent. Opaque enamels block out the metal or foundation they cover.

*Painting Medium*—A liquid with which the enamel is mixed to make paint.

*Pestle*—An implement shaped like a small club, used for grinding enamel in a mortar.

*Pickle*—A chemical solution used for removing oxide scales and impurities from metal. It can be purchased as a noncorrosive compound with instructions on how to use it. Pickle has to be kept in a copper or plastic container only, and only wooden, copper, or plastic tongs should be used to lift objects which have been submerged in pickle.

*Pyrometer*—An instrument used to measure the temperature of the kiln.

*Repoussé*—A technique in which the enamel is deposited onto a metal background that has been shaped into a relief from the reverse side.

*Rouge*—A fine red powder used as a polishing agent for metals.

*Scraper*—A tool with a sharpened edge, used to remove flaws from objects after fusing.

*Screen*—A netlike steel support, on which the work is placed before firing.

*Sgraffito*—A technique of enamel work in which a surface layer of enamel is partially scratched out to reveal the underlying enamel foundation.

*Slush*—A liquid enamel compound, used for certain types of enamel work.

*Snip*—A small strong shears, used for cutting metal and clipping wire.

*Spatula*—A tool consisting of a thin elastic blade with a wooden handle.

*Stilts*—Small supports made from clay or steel which raise the position of enamels in the kiln on a few points only.

*Stylus*—A penlike pointed instrument.

*Tripoli*—A siliceous substance used in powder form for polishing.

# About the Author

MRS. LILI TAUBES is the wife of the distinguished American painter and writer Frederic Taubes. She graduated from the famed School for Applied Art in Vienna, Austria, and later became one of the leading enamel artists of that country. Her work is represented in European museums and also at many exhibitions in the United States.

All materials required can be obtained from: *Allcraft Tool & Supply Co., Inc.*
*22 West 48th Street*
*New York, N.Y.*